FOWL Chicken JOKES to Tickle Your FUNNY BONE

Amelia LaRoche

Enslow Elementary

an imprint of

Enslow Publishers, Inc.
40 Industrial Road
Box 398
Berkeley Heights, NJ 07922
USA

http://www.enslow.com

To Sue—For all the laughs throughout our friendship.

Enslow Elementary, an imprint of Enslow Publishers, Inc.

Enslow Elementary® is a registered trademark of Enslow Publishers, Inc.

Library of Congress Cataloging-in-Publication Data
LaRoche, Amelia.
 Fowl chicken jokes to tickle your funny bone / Amelia LaRoche.
  pages cm. — (Funniest bone animal jokes)
 Includes index.
  Summary: "Read jokes, limericks, tongue twisters, and knock-knock jokes about chickens and other birds. Also find out fun facts about these birds"—Provided by publisher.
 ISBN 978-0-7660-5963-4
 1. Chickens—Juvenile humor. I. Title.
 PN6231.C29L37 2014
 818'.5402—dc23

                    2013008789

Future editions:
Paperback ISBN: 978-0-7660-5964-1   EPUB ISBN: 978-0-7660-5965-8
Single-User PDF ISBN: 978-0-7660-5966-5   Multi-User PDF ISBN: 978-0-7660-5967-2

Printed in the United States of America
072014 HF Group, North Manchester, IN
10 9 8 7 6 5 4 3 2 1

To Our Readers: We have done our best to make sure all Internet addresses in this book were active and appropriate when we went to press. However, the author and the publisher have no control over and assume no liability for the material available on those Internet sites or on other Web sites they may link to. Any comments or suggestions can be sent by e-mail to comments@enslow.com or to the address on the back cover.

Every effort has been made to locate all copyright holders of material used in this book. If any errors or omissions have occurred, corrections will be made in future editions of this book.

Illustration Credits: © Adolfo Medina Licon/iStock/© Thinkstock, p. 10 (middle); © carbouval/iStock/© Thinkstock, p. 28 (top); © chesonya/iStock/© Thinkstock, p. 28 (bottom); Clipart.com, pp. 3 (top), 4 (top), 5 (bottom), 6 (bottom), 7 (top), 9 (top, middle), 11 (top), 12 (bottom), 16 (bottom), 17 (bottom), 18 (top, bottom), 20 (middle), 22 (top), 23 (bottom), 30 (top), 31 (middle), 33 (top), 36 (both), 37 (middle, bottom), 38 (top), 39 (bottom), 40 (left), 41 (middle, gum), 43 (bottom), 45; © dedMazay/ iStock/© Thinkstock, pp. 3 (bottom), 27 (bottom), 31 (bottom); © DrawingDuck/ iStock/© Thinkstock, p. 34 (left); © dues/iStock/© Thinkstock, p. 26 (bottom); Dynamic Graphics/liquidlibrary/© Getty Images/© Thinkstock, pp. 8 (top), 14 (middle), 38 (bottom); © Figura13/ iStock/© Thinkstock, p. 9 (bottom); © Giovanni Banfi/iStock/© Thinkstock, pp. 1, 30 (bottom); © -HeleN-/iStock/© Thinkstock, p. 43 (top); © Igor Zakowski/ iStock/© Thinkstock, p. 25 (bottom), 26 (top); © Julia Kelyukh/iStock/© Thinkstock, p. 21 (bottom); Jupiterimages/ liquidlibrary/© Getty Images/© Thinkstock, pp. 6 (middle), 15 (top); © Liudmila Pantelejenkova/iStock/© Thinkstock, p. 27 (top); © Lorelyn Medina/iStock/© Thinkstock, p. 10 (bottom); © Ma. Luisa Gonzaga/iStock/© Thinkstock, p. 32 (top); © NatuskaDPI/iStock/© Thinkstock, p. 31 (top); © paulili/iStock/© Thinkstock, p. 23 (middle); © Paulo Resende/iStock/© Thinkstock, p. 24 (bottom); © Pedro Guillermo Angeles-Flores/iStock/© Thinkstock, p. 13 (middle); Ralf Hettler/iStock/© Grafissimo/© Thinkstock, p. 5 (top); © retrovectors/iStock, p. 24 (top); © rudall30/iStock/© Thinkstock, pp. 3 (middle), 4 (middle, bottom), 6 (top), 7 (middle), 8 (middle), 11 (middle, bottom), 12 (top), 13 (top, bottom), 14 (bottom), 15 (both at bottom), 16 (top), 17 (top), 18 (middle), 19 (both), 20 (bottom), 21 (top), 22 (bottom), 25 (top), 27 (middle), 29 (bottom), 32 (bottom left, bottom right), 33 (middle, bottom), 34 (right), 35 (both), 37 (top), 38 (middle), 39 (top, middle), 40 (right), 41 (middle, foot), 42 (both), 44 (both); © Smokeyjo/iStock/© Thinkstock, p. 29 (middle).

Cover Illustrations: HitToon.Com/Shutterstock.com (front); © Yael Weiss/iStock/© Thinkstock (back).

Contents

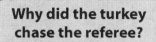 Who Are You Calling Fowl?

Why did the turkey chase the referee?

He was calling a foul.

What do you call a crazy chicken that can tell time?

A cuckoo cluck.

When is the best time to buy chicks?

When they're going cheep.

What do you get when you cross a hen with a duck?

A chicken that lays down.

DID YOU KNOW?

Did you know that *fowl* is the word for certain birds? It's true! A fowl is a bird such as a duck, goose, turkey, or pheasant that is eaten as food or hunted as game.

What do chickens eat for dessert?

Coop-cakes.

What happened to the white duck with messy feathers?

She was tickled pink.

Knock, knock!

Who's there?

Chicken Little.

Chicken Little who?

Chicken Little candle because it's dark out here.

Chickens in chicken coops chatter for chaff.

5

DID YOU KNOW?

If you're a kid, you may have won a "Pullet Surprise" without even knowing it! The story goes that one teacher showed another teacher a paper in which a student wrote, "In 1957, Eugene O'Neill won a Pullet Surprise." The student meant to write "Pulitzer Prize," which is an honor given to great writers. Now some people call the funny mistakes kids make Pullet Surprises. *Pullet* is the word for a young hen.

What did the thief say when the farmer flashed a light into the chicken coop?

"There's nobody here but us chickens!"

Knock, knock!

Who's there?

Fowl.

Fowl who?

Fowl in a mud puddle. Can I use your shower?

An innocent hen was called fowl
By a snobby tree-perching owl.
Said the hen, "In fact,
Your words have no tact,
For your hooting is equally foul!"

The fowl's feathers grew
full in the fall.

In the woods a poor partridge was stunted.
"Let me tell you my story," she grunted.
"Farmer John Tupper
Wants me for supper!
It's too scary to eat while I'm hunted!"

WHAT IS A JOKE?

A good joke is a funny story that makes the person telling it smile. A really good joke makes the person telling it smile and the person hearing it laugh. A great joke makes the person telling it and the person hearing it laugh so hard that the grown-ups in the front seat shout, "If you don't be quiet, we'll turn this car around and drive home right now!" Some jokes feature wordplay, like *foul*, which means "gross and disgusting," versus *fowl*, which is another word for birds that humans use for food.

2 You're Quackers

You're Cordially Invited!

What did the duck serve at his party?

Quackers and cheese.

What did the duck say to the storekeeper when he bought lip balm?

"Put it on my bill."

WHAT IS A LIMERICK?

A limerick is a funny five-line poem. The first two lines and the last line are longer and they rhyme. The third and fourth lines are shorter and rhyme. When you say a limerick out loud, you can hear the rhythm.

What did the duck shout when the ground started to shake?

"Earth quack!"

FUN FACT

Did you know that a duck was given a medal during World War II? It's true! The story is told in a children's book called *Corporal Haggis: The Wartime Story of a Muscovy Duck*. He rode in a British tank, and the friendly, intelligent bird kept the human crew's spirits high during the war.

Why did the duck become an astronaut?

So he could count down.

Why did the duck visit the spider?

Her webbed feet needed repairs.

The rubber duck bobbed in bathtub bubbles.

Why did the duck get in trouble?

He was a wise quacker.

The daring duck's down was plucky!

Limerick

There once was a duck from Duluth
Who thought that he had a loose tooth.
Said his dentist, "I'd drill,
But your tooth is a bill.
Here's my bill for telling the truth!"

Knock, knock!

Who's there?

Duck. Knock, knock!

Who's there?

Duck, duck. Knock, knock!

Who's there?

Duck, duck, goose! You're it!

Why are ducks so smart?

They watch a lot of duckumentaries.

Why did the duck become a comedian?

So she could quack people up.

Limerick

**There once was a duck named Chuck
Who only knew how to cluck.
His lack of a quack
Could be traced right back
To his chicken speech lessons, which stuck.**

FUN FACT

The down on a bird is a layer of fine feathers under the tougher outer feathers. The down keeps the bird warm. Baby birds only have down feathers, which is why they are so fluffy and soft.

Jive Turkeys

Why was turkey served at Thanksgiving?

Because no chickens showed up.

Why do turkeys live in the woods?

Because they can't afford to buy houses.

Where does a 500-pound turkey sit?

Anywhere it wants.

 ## DID YOU KNOW?

Turkeys know each other by their unique voices. Wild turkeys have dozens of noises they use to speak with each other.

What did the mama turkey say to the baby turkey?

"Stop gobbling your food!"

Tricky turkeys tripped teetering turtles.

Why did the turkey laugh?

She heard a funny yolk.

Limerick

The turkeys got into a squabble
Over who had the loudest gobble.
The winner strutted,
The loser muttered,
And his walk turned into a wobble.

DID YOU KNOW?

Did you know that turkeys are even smarter than humans when it comes to learning the lay of the land? It's true! They can memorize the details of an area as big as 1,000 square acres!

Why did the turkey join a band?

Because he had a pair of drumsticks.

Tom Turkey trotted along a treacherous trail.

What do turkeys watch on TV?

The Feather Channel.

Limerick

Did you know that turkeys can fly?
It's true they don't get very high,
But they glide like pros
And land on their toes.
Look up! There's one in the sky!

Knock, knock!

Who's there?

Turkey.

Turkey who?

Turkey wasn't under the mat, so I knocked.

WHAT IS A RIDDLE?

A riddle is a question with an answer that surprises you and makes you laugh. The playful use of words often makes a riddle's answer funny. For instance, try to guess the answer to this question: "Which bird works at construction sites?" It is: "The crane!"

Knock, knock!

Who's there?

Cooper.

Cooper who?

Cooper's full of chickens. Can I sleep in the house?

15

What's Good for the Goose Is Good for the Gander

How do you describe a daring goose?

Plucky!

What happens when geese fall out of the sky?

The rain pours down.

What grows down while it grows up?

A goose.

What do you get when you cross a goose with a movie monster?

Goose-zilla.

FUN FACT

Many types of geese hatch their babies in the north and then migrate south as a family in the winter. Some fly as far as 3,000 miles one way!

Knock, knock!

Who's there?

Gander.

Gander who?

Gander goose come out and play?

Why did the goose honk?

He was stuck in traffic.

What do you get when you cross a goose with a rhinoceros?

A bird that can honk her own horn.

Limerick

Griselda Goose had an old-fashioned gown
That she often wore when she went to town.
The fabric, she said,
Was deep ruby red,
But everyone else could see it was brown.

The huge goose got loose.

When geese fly south, why is one side of the V usually longer than the other?

There are more geese on that side.

A gaggle of geese grazed on grass.

Limerick

In the contest of goose versus gander,
The question was, "Which one is grander?"
The ganders chimed, "We!"
The geese disagreed:
"That claim, sirs, is simply sheer slander!"

FUN FACT

Did you know that a male goose is called a gander, a female is called a goose, and a baby is called a gosling? It's true! Put them all together, and you've got a gaggle of geese.

Knock, knock!

Who's there?

Lucy.

Lucy who?

Lucy goose? Because I found one.

WHAT IS A TONGUE TWISTER?

A tongue twister is a saying that twists your tongue when you try to say it five times as fast as you can!

What do you get when you cross a goose with a balloon?

A fowl ball.

5 This, That, and the Other Bird

The male pheasant's feathers were molting,
Which meant that his looks were revolting:
His wings were patchy,
His chest was scratchy,
Which sent all the hen pheasants bolting.

What kind of bird do you find in the vegetable patch?

A peahen.

FUN FACT

Some geese pair up for life, which can last as long as twenty years for wild geese and more than thirty years for pet geese.

DID YOU KNOW?

Did you know that chickens are the closest living relative of *Tyrannosaurus rex*? It's true! Scientists compared the collagen found in a *T. rex* leg bone with that of modern chickens, and it was almost identical.

Why did the farmer feed gunpowder to his chicks?

He wanted them to become pullets.

Why did the duck hire an accountant?

So he could get de-duck-tions.

What's it called when turkeys fall from the sky?

Fowl weather.

WHAT IS A KNOCK-KNOCK JOKE?

A knock-knock joke is a hard-to-resist call to silliness! When you say, "Knock, knock," the other person has to answer, "Who's there?" For a fun twist, tell a friend you know a great knock-knock joke. Then ask your friend to start it. When your friend says, "Knock, knock," you say, "Who's there?" You'll both get a good laugh!

Knock, knock!

Who's there?

Quack.

Quack who?

Quack open the door and see!

The grumpy grouse's perch was lumpy.

Pretty partridges partied in a pear tree.

Why did the farmer decide not to keep ducks anymore?

He was tired of getting billed for their eggs.

6 Cock-a-Doodle Done

Why did the rooster go to charm school?

To learn his cock-a-doodle-dos from his cock-a-doodle-don'ts!

The retired rooster used to crow cockily.

Why was the rooster always broke?

He worked for chicken feed.

DID YOU KNOW?

Did you know that roosters are loud? It's true! A rooster's crow can be as loud as ninety decibels. Compare that to a vacuum, which *varooms* at about eighty decibels.

What do you get when you cross a rooster with an owl?

All-night crowing.

Knock, knock!

Who's there?

Cocky.

Cocky who?

Cocky doodle do!

How does a rooster keep his feathers tidy?

With his comb.

What was the rooster's least favorite day of the week?

Fry-day.

The red rooster rousted the rabble.

FUN FACT

The red skin on top of a chicken's head is called a comb, and the dangling skin under its beak is called a wattle. The comb and wattle allow a chicken to cool off on hot days. They are larger and more eye-catching on roosters, which use them to attract hens.

Limerick

There once was a chicken named Girard
Who was given the job of coop's guard.
Girard laid an egg—
Her name became Meg—
But she still ran the entire barnyard!

Knock, knock!

Who's there?

Beak.

Beak who?

Be kind to your feathered friends.

There once was a rooster named Drew
Who couldn't cry, "Cock-a-doodle do!"
Try as he might
He sounded a fright—
With no "do" he'd be turned into stew!

What do you call a mean rooster wearing earmuffs?

Whatever you want because he can't hear you.

What do you call a rooster who crows at the same time every morning?

An alarm cluck.

Why did the rooster run away from a fight?

He was chicken!

27

7 EGGS-actly

What does a dizzy hen lay?

Scrambled eggs.

There was a Jersey Giant named Midge
Who moved all of her eggs to the fridge.
When she was asked why,
She said with a sigh,
"They were getting too warm in my plumage!"

DID YOU KNOW?

Did you know that there really is such a thing as green eggs? It's true! Araucana (say: arrow-KAH-nah) chickens lay eggs with pale green shells. They also lay pale blue eggs. The Quetro (KEH-troh) chicken of South America lays pinkish brown eggs. On the inside, all these eggs look like any other eggs, and they taste the same, too.

Knock, knock!

Who's there?

Eggs.

Eggs who?

Eggsactly the right question to ask when a stranger knocks!

What did the hen say when she laid a square egg?

"Ouch!"

What does a sunburned chicken lay?

Fried eggs.

How do you know when the henhouse is too hot?

The chickens lay hard-boiled eggs.

The hens huddled near a mud puddle.

29

Knock, knock!

Who's there?

Egg yolk.

Egg yolk who?

Egg yolk's not funny if you have to egg-splain it.

How do dogs like their eggs served?

Pooched.

What did the hen say to the farmer who wanted her egg?

"Beat it!"

The farmer begged for eight eggs.

Limerick

Biddy the hen laid two speckled eggs.
She kept them warm between her legs.
When they started to crack,
She jumped high and back.
Out peeped her babies: Mumbles and Pegs!

FUN FACT

More and more people are buying "cage-free" eggs. They don't want to buy eggs from chickens that live on battery farms, where the cages are so tiny and cramped the hens can't even stretch their wings. These people look for egg cartons with the Cage-Free or Free-Range label.

What do you get when a hen lays an egg on a hill?

An eggroll.

Eight beige eggs were laid in a cage.

The hen incubated her eggs under her legs.

Knock, knock!

Who's there?

Omelet.

Omelet who?

Omelet you know as soon as you open the door!

What destroyed the chicken coop?

An eggs-plosion.

What's a chicken's favorite vegetable?

Eggplant.

DID YOU KNOW?

Did you know that chicks can count? It's true! Scientists in Italy set up two screens in front of baby chickens and then moved balls back and forth behind the screens. The chicks were able to keep track of which screen had the most balls behind it!

What do chicken families do on summer afternoons?

The go on peck-nics.

Why did the chicken coop have two doors?

If it had four, it would be a sedan.

What do you call a chicken after it's a year old?

Two years old.

What was the name of the movie about the time-traveling chicken?

Beak to the Future.

How did the chicken get into college?

She passed the hen-trance exam.

A smart cluck stuck to his flock.

Limerick
Some kinds of fowl are smarter than you think.
Some can fly faster than people can blink.
They recall faces,
They map out places,
And when you tell them a joke, they may wink!

FUN FACT

Chickens live in stable social groups, with each chicken knowing its place in the "pecking order." They can recognize and remember at least one hundred other chickens.
They use more than thirty types of sounds to tell each other things, like, "Yum, there are tasty grubs here!" Or "Hide! There's a hawk flying overhead!"

Knock, knock!

Who's there?

Henny.

Henny who?

Henny one in there?

The husky hen befriended a dusky wren.

Why did the chicken go to the bank?

She needed help balancing her chick-book.

9 Going South

Knock, knock!

Who's there?

Duck.

Duck who?

Duck! Geese are flying overhead!

The high-flying flock flew through flurries.

Why do geese fly in a V?

It's too hard to fly in a Q.

Why do geese fly south in the winter?

It's too far to walk.

DID YOU KNOW?

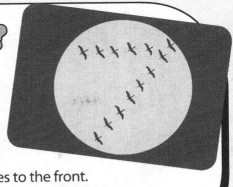

Did you know that migrating geese fly in a V formation, called a skein, to save energy? It's true! The birds in the front reduce air pressure on the birds in the back. They take turns going first. When a bird gets tired, he or she falls to the back of the V and a new bird moves to the front. Military planes sometimes fly in a V to save fuel, but geese came up with the idea long before humans did.

Why don't ducks like frozen ponds?

Because their feet are too small for ice skates!

Knock, knock!

Who's there?

Lettuce.

Lettuce who?

Lettuce fly south, because winter's here!

Why don't geese use a compass to fly south?

They can't hold a compass and fly at the same time.

Migrating takes much muscle.

Limerick

Some words have two meanings, like *goose*.
The difference is plain to deduce:
One has wings and can fly,
Upon eggs it does lie;
The other is painful pinching abuse.

Why shouldn't you look up in the fall?

That's when geese are flying south!

Bar-headed geese in Asia migrate over the Himalaya mountain range—even over Mount Everest, which is 29,029 feet high. The air there can be freezing cold, but that doesn't stop these amazing flyers!

Which day of the week do geese migrate?

Fly-day.

If fruit comes from a fruit tree, where do chickens come from?

A poul-tree.

Limerick

**The goose began honking and squawking.
The coop's seams were not filled with caulking.
When winter air blew,
His poor feathers flew—
The subzero gale was too shocking!**

10 Crossing the Road

Why did the chicken cross the road?

To get to the other side.

The trained bird's brain was ingrained to gain grain.

DID YOU KNOW?

Did you know that chickens have self-control? It's true! Scientists in England tested hens with colored buttons. When a hen pecked the right button, she got a food reward. If the hen waited three seconds, she received a small amount of food. But if she waited for twenty-two seconds, she got a "jackpot" of food. Once the hens figured out the test, they all waited for the jackpot more than 90 percent of the time!

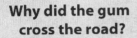

Why did the gum cross the road?

It was stuck to the chicken's foot.

Why did the duck waddle across the road?

It was the chicken's day off.

Why did the hen cross only half the road?

She wanted to lay it on the line.

Knock, knock!

Who's there?

Interrupting chicken.

Interrupting chick—

CLUCK!

Why did the partridge cross the road?

To prove he wasn't a chicken!

Limerick
The chicken, we're told, crossed the road.
When asked why he did that, he crowed,
"The reason is plain:
I go for the grain!"
And off to the silo he strode.

FUN FACT

There are about 20 billion chickens in the world. That means there are more of them than any other type of bird. There are dozens of chicken breeds, from the tiny Serama, which stands only six inches high, to the large, friendly, thirteen-pound Jersey Giant.

Why did the dinosaur cross the road?

Because the chicken hadn't evolved yet.

Knock, knock!

Who's there?

Henways.

Henways who?

Henways about five pounds.

Gentle intelligent hens are our friends.

Why did the chicken stop crossing the road?

So people would stop making jokes about why the chicken crossed the road!

Why did the vampire chicken cross the road?

To get to the dark side.

Limerick

There once was a rooster named Chuck
Who the farmer said had good luck.
Said Chuck, "A birdbrain?
That hardly pertains,
For I am far more than just a dumb cluck!"

Make a Fowl Flipbook

HERE'S WHAT YOU WILL NEED:

- a stack of paper
- a pen or pencil

DIRECTIONS:

1. Get a stack of paper. You can use sticky notes, a school notebook, or just a stack of scrap paper. The bigger your stack of paper, the more animated your flipbook will be.

2. Decide the action you want to show. You can draw a chicken crossing the road, or a chick hatching out of an egg.

3. Decide what the "start" picture will look like and what the "end" picture will look like. Once you've drawn your "start" picture in the bottom corner of the first piece of paper, redraw it on the next page, with just a slight difference that makes it closer to the "end" picture. With every picture you draw, make it look a little more like the "end" picture. Keep drawing pictures in the bottom corner of each page until you get to the "end" picture.

4. Put the pages in order so that the "start" drawing is on the top of the pile and the "end" drawing is on the bottom.

5. Once you're done drawing at least twenty-five pictures, flip the pages rapidly with your thumb and watch your flipbook come alive!

Words to Know

chaff—The outer layer of wheat grain.

collagen—Part of the tissue of an animal.

decibel—A unit of measure for noise.

identical—Exactly the same.

incubate—To keep eggs warm (under a chicken or in a heated box called an incubator) until they hatch; it takes a chick about 21 days to develop inside the egg and then hatch.

joke—Something that is said to make people laugh.

limerick—An amusing poem in which the first, second, and fifth lines rhyme, and the shorter third and fourth lines rhyme.

memorize—To learn something by heart.

molt—To lose feathers.

peahen—A female peacock.

plumage—A bird's feathers.

poultry—Birds such as chickens that are kept for meat or eggs.

pullet—A hen that is less than a year old.

revolting—Gross or disgusting.

slander—To say something bad and untrue about someone else.

tongue twister—A series of fun words that can be hard to say out loud.

Read More

Books

Arnold, Terry, et al. *Why Did the Chicken Cross the Road?* New York: Dial, 2006.

Keller, Charles. *Giggle Fit: Animal Jokes*. New York: Sterling Publishing, 2004.

National Geographic Kids. *Just Joking: 300 Hilarious Jokes, Tricky Tongue Twisters, and Ridiculous Riddles*. Des Moines, Iowa: National Geographic Children's Books, 2012.

Internet Addresses

Aha! Jokes: Animal Jokes
http://www.ahajokes.com/animal_jokes_for_kids.html

Ducksters: Bird Jokes
http://www.ducksters.com/jokesforkids/birds.php

Squigly's Playhouse: Chicken Jokes and Riddles
http://www.squiglysplayhouse.com/JokesAndRiddles/chicken.html

Index